Boys I Us...

A collection of Haiku

Heather L Barnes

Heather L Barnes

I am so grateful
My life is blessed because you
have made an entrance

June
2016

Published By Red Squid Publishing

www.redsquidpublishing.com

For permission requests, contact the publisher at:

Red Squid Publishing
P.O. Box 80125
Lincoln, NE 68501

www.redsquidpublishing.com.

ISBN 978-0-9973600-0-4
First Edition, April 2016

Dedication

Dedicated to all the boys I used to know...

Special Thanks

Anthony Rendel, without you this book would not be a thing. Your willingness to do all the detail work that I am awful at turned a bunch of random haikus into an actual thing. I could never have done the thing without you. You help make all things possible.

Isa Ledo, you truly are my ASLP. You have been there for all of the ridiculous, the laughter, and the tears. You were sent the first poem long before the idea of collecting them into a book and you know where all the bodies are buried.

Faith McKay, you are one of the strongest and most amazing women I know. You continuously inspire me to chase after my dreams and remind me with a properly prioritized list, anything is possible. (She's a fantastic author, too. Seriously, go look her up online.)

Cei Loofe, you were the first person to call me a poet. You continuously offer me life perspective I would be a hot mess without. You inspire me to own my creative self.

Michelle Walsh, you are my biggest, loudest cheerleader! Seriously lady, you are my heart!

Table of Contents

Introduction

At this point in my life I always figured I would have it more together, especially in the arena of dating. Don't misunderstand me, I am not wanting to be on the fast track for the white picket fence. I just assumed by this point I would have found a decent person who I rather enjoy getting naked with who gets as excited about $5 movies on Tuesdays as I do. Instead I have bumbled around in the world of "What the hell are you thinking..." and "What the hell am I thinking..."

Writing haikus about bad dates, bad boyfriends, or bad situations became a way to deal with the bumps and bruises along the way. It was a way to break down a situation into its simplest elements, 17 syllables at a time, smile and laugh about it.

All the haikus in the book are about boys that I did in fact "used to know" and, yes, some of them I knew biblically. Not all, though. This collection includes boys that didn't make it past the first date, boys that became casual or even serious boyfriends, and some boys that I am still friends with today.

I can honestly say that all of them served a purpose in my life. They worked to show me a clearer picture of myself, what I was capable of, and, perhaps most importantly, what I deserve. Not to mention, without them you wouldn't be reading this book right now.

So sit back, grab a glass of wine (you might need it), and enjoy the beautiful art form of haiku as applied to the incredibly bumpy road of my dating life.

And so it begins...

To everyone who

Didn't have a beard, or shaved:

You didn't know me.

To everyone who

Had a beard while we dated:

You are my favorite.

Dates...

You came in all black;

I can't tell if that's a skirt–

Hail, Prince of Darkness!

Met for dinner date.

Conversation was so poor,

Left with no pizza.

Wait! Something is wrong...

I think I saw it again–

Are you missing teeth?

"You own books? That's weird.

You don't, like, read them do you?

You're a girl who reads?!"

Known you five minutes

Brother's exploded food tube

Please do not tell me

Woodchipper, you have

Weird looks you gave when I asked

What all have you chipped?

Talk in this movie,

I will cut you with a knife.

I hate you right now.

Dating just two weeks

Insurance is not a gift

Just get me flowers

A woodland creature,

Puffy cheeks so chipmunk like–

Stay married, give thanks

Asked for my number

Used it to text, "have a wife"

Keeping it classy

It wasn't me,

It was you...

Fifteen, I knew you

But we did not make the sex

You left me for it

All the years have passed

My mom still loves you the best

Yearly life updates

A football player

I thought we could be in love

But you were so dumb

His hair said it all

He had stupid floppy hair

This could not end well

Hadn't heard from you

Self-inflicted gun to chest

Glad we could catch up

Shared love of comics

A Dominatrix I'm not

True love wasn't found

Of course you love me

Of course I don't seem to care

Of course you will cry

You lived far away

I feel that was for the best

Made your stalking hard

You were an asshole

Abusive and a big jerk

Yet, your mom blamed me

You were not quite right

My name you carved on your thigh

Not love, just scary

You are a grown-up

As cool for you as that is

I'm not, have to pass

You cried all the time

I didn't know how to deal

Here's Kleenex, be gone

You said you loved me

For the first time in a list

Along with chicken

Snore so loud I weep

Sleep Apnea for the win

You don't need to breathe

Oh, Sleep Apnea

A CPAP is not sexy

We must be apart

Norse God I made you

Version of you in my head

Better than real life

It might have
been me...

You were very sad

Why wouldn't I try to fix?!

I am a moron

This one was my fault

No one I can blame but me

Ugly married guy

There were lots of cows

When did I think that was good?

Moving on was best

When life was choppy

My anchor I could count on

But please set me free

You liked me too soon

My like of you came too late

Now you have ten kids

Sexy time...

If you were concerned

He would try to sleep with me,

Pick better best friends

Down in the basement

You put moves on me that day

On your grandma's couch

Saying "Shipping Out"

Does not guarantee access

To my lady parts

Telling me that you

Like to have sex with fat girls

Won't get me naked

When sexting with me

"Crotch" shouldn't be used, ever

Like, never ever

Dick pics are no fun

'Til something small your way comes–

Banana for scale

You had a big truck

I was sad to discover

The only big thing

Having a penis

Is only helpful to me

If it is working

Wait, that is my leg.

Not technically Doggie Style.

Please, just stop. Headache.

Not sure where you learned

That "sex move" but honestly

Don't bite someone's clit

You came with no skills

Sex had never been so bad!

Glad you listen well

Legos, lots of art...

Things that I have collected–

Can't forget V-Cards

Dating P.S.A...

Guys with beards are nice

Goatees are not trustworthy

Dating PSA

Short story written

Trying to woo me should not

Include word "armpit"

So you have a cat

And you guys have matching clothes

Don't date dudes with cats

Telling everyone

My boyfriend you thought you'd be

Doesn't make it so

In conclusion...

A few of the boys

That I have known, I have loved

To those boys, thank you

About the Author

Heather Barnes is a native of southwest Michigan. She now lives in Lincoln, Nebraska, where she graduated from the University of Nebraska - Lincoln, majoring in English as well as film studies. She has enjoyed her time in Nebraska, but misses Lake Michigan every day. Though a self-described hopeless romantic, Heather does not blame Disney Princess culture for setting unrealistic expectations for dating. Instead, she shakes her fist angrily at DC & Marvel for that. When she is not pining away for a brooding hero, she spends her days writing poetry or working on other artistic endeavors, in addition to being involved in the spoken word/slam poetry community. Find the author online at www.artistofwords.com

Made in the USA
Charleston, SC
12 May 2016